BRITAIN IN PICTURES
THE BRITISH PEOPLE IN PICTURES

THE LIBERAL PARTY

MR. GLADSTONE TRAVELLING IN A BUS
Water colour by Alfred Morgan, 1884

THE
LIBERAL PARTY

R. J. CRUIKSHANK

*WITH
4 PLATES IN COLOUR
AND
19 ILLUSTRATIONS IN
BLACK & WHITE*

COLLINS · 14 ST. JAMES'S PLACE · LONDON
MCMXLVIII

PRODUCED BY
ADPRINT LIMITED LONDON

PRINTED IN GREAT BRITAIN BY
CLARKE & SHERWELL LTD NORTHAMPTON
ON MELLOTEX BOOK PAPER MADE BY
TULLIS RUSSELL & CO LTD MARKINCH SCOTLAND

LIST OF ILLUSTRATIONS

PLATES IN COLOUR

BLACK AND WHITE ILLUSTRATIONS

*The Editor is most grateful to all those who have so kindly helped in the selection of illustrations,
especially to officials of the various public Museums, Libraries and Galleries, and to all others
who have generously allowed pictures and MSS. to be reproduced*

INTRODUCTION

PEOPLE on the whole are very civil and obliging to Liberals nowadays —at least in public. How times have changed! When this writer was a small boy in the days of the last Liberal Government, quite nice, rosy Conservatives threatened to hang Ministers on lamp-posts, and there were Shelleyan Socialists who promised that at the coming revolution their first tumbril would be reserved, not for Tories, but for Liberals. In those days, Lloyd George used to tell a story of a man who saved a stranger from drowning at risk to his own life. Presented with a medal by the Mayor, the hero said diffidently, "I did only what any other Englishman would have done in my place. I first turned him over to make sure he wasn't Lloyd George, then I dragged him out of the water."

To-day, when there are only ten Liberal members of the House of Commons, almost every Conservative, and many Socialists, will display on very slight provocation what Mr. Herbert Morrison calls "his Liberal streak." There are two historic strands in Liberalism—the care for liberty, and the drive towards social justice. To combine the two, to achieve the one without sacrificing the other, is the object of a Liberal society. The Conservative suitor to-day approaches the Liberal as an ally in the struggle for Freedom. Labour woos him on his reformist side, saying, "We are the inheritors of the last Liberal Government. We are completing your grand design of Radical Reform. You cannot escape the law of political Evolution. A Liberal of 1910 must either be a Socialist in 1948 or become extinct." At this point, one hears the mellow voice of Lord Woolton calling, "Ah, my dear fellow, Codlin's the friend, not Short." Lord Woolton is at pains to present the Conservative Party of to-day as dedicated to preserving the Liberal heritage of Freedom. At Birmingham, in March 1947, for example, he said, "There is a great liberal sentiment in this country. There is now no major issue between Liberalism and Conservatism. *They are both expressions of the same political philosophy*, and those old battles that used to enliven political life in the days gone by, between Liberals and Tories, are now just ancient and meaningless feuds." After that, Codlin seems about to go off arm-in-arm with Little Nell, but is arrested by the Lord President of the Council genially declaring, "Short's your man. You know old Short. *He* won't let you down."

This solicitude is very pleasant, but the simple truth about the impenitent Liberal is that he has no desire to become absorbed by either Conservatism or Socialism. It may be sheer contrariness on his part, but he honestly thinks that the other Parties are too closely tied to special interests to be truly representative of the community. The influence of big business on Conservative policy and the influence of the Trade Unions on Labour Policy are both too strong for his liking. He finds Conservatism negative, living in the past, and lacking the positive qualities needed to arrest the drift towards the total State. Above all, its record in foreign policy and in domestic affairs, in the years between the wars, makes him very distrustful.

As for Socialism, the Liberal is less attracted by it now that he has seen it in power, than when it was a dream of noble minds. He feels that his old suspicion that Democratic Socialism is really a contradiction in terms has been confirmed. State control over wide areas of the national life cannot, he thinks, be imposed without destroying certain essential freedoms which he values more than security. He sees the Liberal influences inside the Labour Party daily losing ground to the doctrinaires and the Marxists. Twenty years ago, and less, what a roar of old Radical protest would have come from the Party at the thought of imposing direction of labour in peace-time!

It may be a physical weakness of Liberalism to-day that it is not based on any concentration of economic power. But its corresponding advantage is that it is free from sectional loyalties; it is not tied to any interests. It can bring the same critical spirit to bear upon the activities of Monopolies as upon Trade Unions, upon Trade Associations as upon that formidable new group of masters, the managers and the technical experts. It can speak for that almost forgotten man, the consumer. Wouldn't any thoughtful Conservative or Socialist agree that this is a good thing, in the country's interest?

So long ago as the election of 1918, the pundits were saying that the Liberal Party was dead, and all that was needed was to find its rightful heirs, and distribute its inheritance. Yet, through these thirty years, nothing is more remarkable in our politics than the existence and persistence of an indestructible core of Liberal votes. Many setbacks and disappointments have been sustained. There have been schisms, there have been desertions, but the Party has remained vigorously alive, and the organised expression of Liberal opinion has never failed to make itself felt. There are at least three million Liberal voters in the country to-day—possibly the figure is nearer four million. The Liberal believes that his political faith is rooted in the national temperament; that Britain is Liberal at heart. He believes that Liberalism has a very great part yet to play in the world of political ideas and of political action. And he is certain that the effectiveness of Liberalism depends upon its continuing independence.

The pages that follow give a rapid sketch of the Liberal Party's history, touching principally upon the ideas that informed it, the ideals that inspired it. The writer's object is to show how Liberalism came to be not a

8

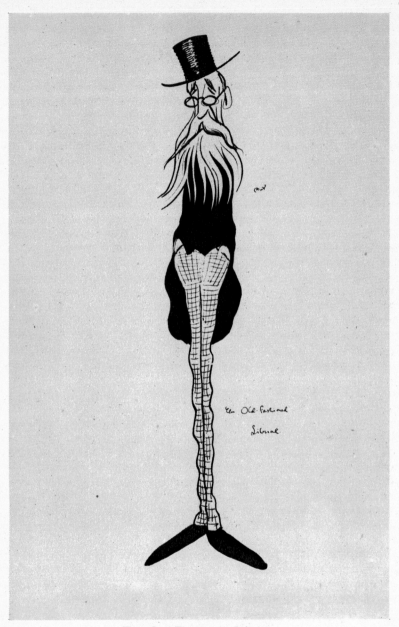

THE OLD-FASHIONED LIBERAL
Cartoon by Sir Max Beerbohm

middle way between Conservatism and Socialism, but a different way. Liberalism is a political philosophy of moderation and reason, a creed that detests violence, compulsion and authoritarianism, but it finds its driving force in the impulse towards social justice. It refuses to believe in the inevitability of the class war. It is suspicious of intuitions and "the fantasia of the unconscious" in politics. It believes that tolerance and good sense do finally justify themselves in human affairs; that truth has everything to gain and nothing to fear from open debate; and that tyranny, no matter how dynamic and efficient it is, is self-destructive. First and foremost, the Liberal Party is the party of Freedom. The main debates and main struggles in which it has been engaged for more than a century have revolved around the issue which concerns us all very much to-day—"What is Liberty? What are its frontiers?" We may know well enough what freedom of opinion and freedom of religion are. They are clear to see. But social freedoms, economic freedoms, where do they begin and leave off? Our deepest problems of to-day are not new. In our great-grandfathers' times, thoughtful men and women were absorbed by the questions that occupy the modern politician and leader-writer:—How to equate freedom and the forms of collective planning. How to reconcile a well-organised society with the full expression of the individual, particularly the uncommon individual. How to achieve security without enduring regimentation. How to set free the vital energies of the whole people.

The history of the Liberal Party is, then, really the history of the evolution of the Idea of Freedom in modern society. Liberalism has always put great store upon the *uniqueness* of the individual, upon the value of personality, upon the private conscience and the private judgment. It isn't hard to see how those recognitions might at one period lead a Party to lay emphasis on personal freedom and resistance to the repressive, paralysing authority of the State, and, at another period, to lay emphasis upon collective social action to redress injustice, to protect the weak and to set free the energies of the people. This attempt to maintain the balance of rights and duties has involved debate, controversy and sometimes almost unresolvable dilemmas. But it has prevented dictatorship or revolution. Liberalism at its best has always been a conscious effort to achieve the just society through stabilising a delicate equilibrium of freedom and obligation. The Party has had its failures and shortcomings. But, if we believe that the chief value of history is the light it throws upon man's behaviour as a political animal, then the experiences of a century and more of British Liberalism should have a very real interest for us to-day. Not the least, one would suppose, for the young—who must be rather bemused by modern politics.

CHARLES JAMES FOX, 1749-1806
Water colour by Lady Diana Beauclerk

THE BEGINNINGS

HOW did the Liberal Party begin? In one sense, it never began. It was a continuation. Before it became a party, it was (as Birrell used to say) a state of mind. There are those who find the origins of British Liberalism in the days of Oliver Cromwell and the struggle with the Stuarts. If, on the other hand, you are a Tory, you may be inclined to agree with Dr. Johnson that Satan, the leader of the celestial Opposition, was the first Whig. The first politicians to be called Liberals in this country were the immediate heirs of the Whigs of the eighteenth century—or, to put it more truthfully, of Charles James Fox's New Whigs. They had no

11

reason to be ashamed of this ancestry. From the Whigs the Liberals derived their principles of toleration, of emancipation, and of resistance to the arbitrary power of government. The principles of the Foxites are often thought of as the negative side of Liberalism. Plainly a just society cannot be built simply on a protest. But a society in which the old Whig protest against arbitrary power ceases to be heard is no longer a free society.

The name of Liberal was first used as a scornful joke, and that, indeed, is the way in which a great many honourable and famous names have originated. In the early years of the nineteenth century the men of Spain who fought for their country's liberties called themselves *Liberales*. In France, the supporters of the popular movement called themselves *Libéraux*. They were moderate enough liberties that these men struggled for, constitutional guarantees mainly. In Spain, they sought a monarch of their own choosing, and the end of the Inquisition. But to the High Tories of that age, the friends of liberty always looked funny as well as disreputable, like the comic brigands in an *opéra bouffe*. Liberal, therefore, seemed a heaven-sent nickname to apply first to the Whigs, and then to those early Tory Reformers, the followers of George Canning. The word possessed all the qualities to be looked for in an effective label of British political abuse, for it sounded Continental, disloyal, and agnostic. Its success may be judged from its effect upon George IV. His Majesty, writing to Charles Williams Wynn in 1825, was at once put in mind of the French Revolution. The name recalled to the King "the deplorable revolutionary sentiment" that was abroad in England in the 1790's, "when it required all the talent and firmness of Mr. Pitt to put it down."

Let us look at the setting of this period when Liberalism was born. They were cheerless years that followed Waterloo. Times were hard in the cities, labourers went hungry in the shires, there were many walking scarecrows on the roads. The Corn Law of 1815 brought dearer bread at a time when work was scarce. The working people suffered the hardships of the Industrial Revolution long before they enjoyed its benefits. What was most depressing of all, there seemed no hope of change in the social and political order. The narrowest, harshest and most bigoted Conservatism prevailed. In the frozen society of that time, fear played on fear; hate returned hate; and any show of discontent brought sterner repression.

Yet while England seemed to be bound in the hardest of political winters, there, under the ice and snow, the seeds of a new time were germinating. Political persecution created an interest in every political heresy. Decay in the Church set men thinking about the mysterious destiny of their souls. The sloth of the Universities gave learning the spice of illicit pleasure. Reading was seldom pursued with greater fervour than when pamphleteers and printers were being tried at Newgate, and when there was a crushing tax on newspapers. Speculations about the origin of Government, about the relation of man to society, about natural rights and civil rights, about pantheism, atheism, feminism, socialism, communism, and the recasting of all institutions were followed with rapt eagerness.

Its critics like to point out that at many stages in its history the Liberal Party has been a variegated party. It resembles the Church of England in this, that its umbrella has been spread over High thinkers, Low thinkers and very Broad thinkers. But never at any time was the name Liberal assumed with so much enthusiasm by such a diversity of God's creatures as during the early part of the nineteenth century. By the time the crowds were gathering around the market cross and on the moor to shout for the Reform Bill, there were as many persuasions of Liberals as there are religions in the State of California. To begin with, there were the sons of Rousseau and Tom Paine. Those spirits that had caught fire long ago from the French Revolution now experienced a renewal of hope. They had never lost faith in the natural goodness of man. Once he had been freed from thraldom to kings and priests, his capacity for growth in wisdom and virtue was measureless. "Man is born free and he is everywhere in chains," said Rousseau. Now was the time to renew the struggle to break those chains. Then there were those—poor men mainly, villagers and mechanics—who had found a peerless champion in William Cobbett, the "People's hero." He had begun life as an old English Tory and ended it as an old English Radical. Cobbett's "Political Register," read eagerly in the cottages and taverns, was perhaps the most effective popular journalism ever written. What exhilarating reading he makes to-day! His words rain down like blows. He carries a big stick with which he lays about him most joyously, bringing it down on the backs of the bad landlords, the financiers, speculators and jobbers, the "tax-eaters," and all his other pet aversions. Cobbett had no political system, but he had a great love for the poor. He had no coherent doctrine, but he had a thundering anger in his soul against injustice. He saw politics, as Kean acted Shakespeare, by flashes of lightning. Cobbett stands for an old English strain which, pray God, may not die out among us—the Radical without a theory, but with a noble wrath. Then there were the working-men's associations that were the forerunners of the modern Trade Unions. They drew inspiration from such characters as Robert Owen and Francis Place. Owen saw that there were other causes besides kings and aristocracies for the human predicament. This successful cotton spinner, who was both a Socialist and an autocrat, was a century ahead of his time in his faith in the power of good working conditions, fair wages and education to transform men and women, physically and morally. The leadership of that tailor of genius, Francis Place—the "man behind the scenes," the beneficent wire-puller—who by unwearying effort secured the repeal of Pitt's Combination Act (the Act which made it criminal for workmen to band together to protect their interests), showed what well-planned agitation could accomplish in redressing injustice. There were deists and atheists in this grand alliance that was formed against

13

Conservatism in the 'twenties, but there were many more who were drawn to the popular side by their religious feelings. The "Tolpuddle Martyrs," for example, were men with a deep faith in God that sustained them through their trials. The Nonconformists had been shut out from the public service and from the Universities, and the Repeal of the Test Act in 1829 brought only a partial relief from their disabilities. The treatment by Church and State of Methodists, Baptists, Congregationalists, Unitarians and the other dissenting bodies produced *The Chapel Militant*, that unique feature of British politics. Dissenting Ministers, who conceived of Church and State in the images of John Bunyan, were strange allies for the Liberal Whig aristocrats, urbane, sceptical, cosmopolitan; with their fine taste in pictures, wines and the Roman poets; their reverence for French civilisation, and their love of horses; their fondness for the card table; their wit. Yet the links between Brooks's Club and Sion Chapel were to endure a very long time. During a hundred years there were to be found no more loyal and constant friends of the Liberal cause in good times and bad than the Nonconformists.

Then there were the Utilitarians. These were the men of cool, investigating minds to whom no institution, however venerable, was sacred. They tapped everything with their little hammers, asking, "Is it useful? Does it work? Is it worth what it costs?" These hammers tapped insistently at the worm-eaten furniture and the rusty machinery of the State in George IV's time. Parliament, the Law, the Church, the Universities—nothing was left unexamined by these diligent inspectors. "It is the greatest happiness of the greatest number that is the measure of right and wrong." This was the renowned principle laid down by the founder of the Utilitarian school, Jeremy Bentham. What holes have been picked in that theory since! But Bentham's copious, fertile, incessantly inquisitive intellect proved an invaluable instrument of social change. The influence of Bentham united with the influence of Adam Smith to create the Manchester School of Liberalism. The Manchester School—that seems a grisly name nowadays! It stands for the politics of Scrooge. But to many honest men at that time *laissez-faire* came as the revelation of an immense beneficence. Adam Smith's *Wealth of Nations* had been published in 1776, the year when Britain's mercantile policies led to the revolt of the American Colonies. The *Wealth of Nations* was like one of those great novels which change the world's fashion in heroes. In the place of the soldier, the aristocrat, the gallant or the man of sensibility, the age was presented with the merchant hero, an adventurous young giant, full of enterprise and resource. He was, in Lecky's account of him, "a robust, healthy, and self-reliant type, extremely jealous of Government interference, extremely tenacious of individual liberty." By his energy, industry, inventiveness and risk-taking, this self-reliant hero would make, not only himself, but his fellow-citizens rich and happy. The individualist was the true public benefactor. The nation's

POLITICAL MEETING AT BIRMINGHAM TO URGE THE ADOPTION OF THE REFORM BILL, 1832
Oil painting by Benjamin Robert Haydon, 1786-1846

welfare was best served when everybody was hard at work pursuing his private benefit. To the rising class of middle-class industrialists this became a revelation of truth confirmed in their daily life. This was *their* ideal of Liberalism.

One can recognise the lineal descendants of some of these types of the early years of the nineteenth century among a representative Liberal group to-day, particularly in the towns of the South and West of England. There one meets the patrician whose ancestor was one of Charles James Fox's lambs and who makes it a point of traditional pride to support whatever is the most advanced view in the Party at any given moment. There is the Nonconformist minister, steeped in Bunyan, Baxter and John Wesley, sometimes an exponent of "the dissidence of dissent," sometimes filled with a Celtic glow of evangelism. There is the schoolmaster or the tailor who still reads Tom Paine and holds a half-romantic, half-rationalist view of man's perfectibility. There is the angry Radical working-man who has the blood of William Cobbett in his veins and is against all institutions, seeing them as heartless, soulless monsters. He rails against public Boards and the planned Society, as his grandfather railed against the Poor Law, the Church and the squires. Then there is the spiritual heir of Adam Smith for whom Free Trade is a moral issue even more than an economic one ; he is often a Scot, with a strong vein of granitic Aberdeen principle in him. These characters are Liberals because there is nothing else they can be.

But to return to the 'thirties. The clamour for Reform, in which all these voices blended, grew ever louder and more threatening. In those exciting "six days of May," 1831, the storm rose so high that King William feared it would shake the crown from his head. If Reform were denied, then blood would flow. But victory was won, and it was a famous victory, the opposition surrendering unconditionally at the end. But among those many groups and elements who made up the grand alliance there was no agreement as to what the Reform Bill meant. To the Radicals it was the beginning of a new social order. To its Conservative supporters, such men as Stanley and Graham, it was an insurance against revolution. To the middle classes Reform meant the achievement of deferred political power. To business men it represented the triumph of Manchester and Birmingham over Old Sarum and the rotten boroughs. So many hopes, so many illusions, so much oratory, so many cheers—and, inevitably, so many disappointments! Though right honourable and honourable gentlemen continued to use the name of Whig for twenty years after the Reform Bill, we may fairly regard 1832 as the year of the birth of the Liberal Party. But it was in the disillusions that followed Reform far more than in its achievement that modern Liberalism really began.

WHIG-LIBERALS

DISAPPOINTMENT came speedily. Reform was won, but poor Jo was still being moved on. The new towns had been enfranchised, but little relief had come to the serfs in mills and mines. The constitutional revolution had taken place, but the black spots of the Industrial Revolution remained. One of the Whig Government's earliest acts was to put down the "rising of the peasants" in the Southern counties, and they did so with the unfeeling hardness of men of property in a panic. For the under-dog, what had changed? Some things, indeed, had apparently changed for the worse. The New Poor Law, the pride of the Utilitarians, brought an outcry from Radical and Tory alike. The benevolent figure of Jeremy Bentham was seen to be casting a shadow. That shadow was Bumble. And the child of the new enlightenment turned out to be Oliver Twist, the starved charity boy. Wherever the greatest happiness of the greatest number was to be found in Britain, it was certainly not in the model workhouses. Something, too, had gone wrong with the fine theory of Adam

THE REFORM BILL RECEIVING THE KING'S ASSENT BY ROYAL COMMISSION, 1832
Engraving by William Walker, 1836

Smith that the general interest was best served through the exercise of the unfettered self-interest of the business man. There might be hearty agreement with this proposition on the Cotton Exchange and in Lombard Street. But the theory was not at all confirmed by life in the back streets of, say, Manchester or Merthyr Tydfil, or in the Dorset villages. The heart-aching delays of·the Ten Hours Bill convinced many working-men they had as little to hope from their new masters as from their old.

One consequence of the great disillusion was the birth of Chartism in 1837. To the Chartists, the remedy for the future of Reform was obvious. It was more Reform. Complete Reform. One man, one vote. Then the House of Commons would be a true instrument of social justice. So the People's Charter called for universal suffrage, the secret ballot, annual Parliaments, payment of M.P.s, abolition of the property qualification, and equal electoral districts.

Chartism drew into itself the Radicalism of the working-men's associations and the warm-hearted anarchism of Cobbett. The break with the other groups, the aristocratic Whigs and the middle-class Liberals, who had acted together in the agitation for Reform, seemed complete. The demands of the Charter were moderation indeed; but the flame of Chartism was revolutionary. Reading the accounts of the Chartist meetings, dipping into their newspapers, one feels that this is the certain start of a Victorian third party. One turns with eagerness the next dozen pages of history expecting the story of the rise of a militant Socialist movement—a movement that would surely become irresistible by the 'fifties. The classic conditions for revolutionary change seemed at hand. In 1832, the middle classes had seized power from the landed aristocracy; now there was a far more formidable dispossessed class, burning with grievances, gathering its forces in a score of cities and towns, and·it would soon be marching on London from every part of the kingdom. Yet within a little more than ten years from its birth, the Chartist movement, with all its power and passion, had come to an end, leaving only a great angry glow in the sky. This was in part because times were getting better, but, more than this, because the Anti-Corn-Law League had arisen to provide a new and exciting cause to unite rich men and poor, a cause dear to Victorian hearts, for it combined the prospect of material good with the satisfaction of moral passion. The Ten Hours Bill was, in the end, carried in 1847, a year before the last great Chartist demonstration, the meeting on Kennington Common which caused the Duke of Wellington to stand on guard for the revolution that never happened.

Revolutionaries are often cheated out of their revolutions in Britain, because the old governing class, its wary eye cocked for every change in the political weather, takes over the leadership of the dispossessed class when it is on the point of seizing power. This principle of the adaptation of the British governing class is one which Victorian Marxists, as well as

THE LAST WORD

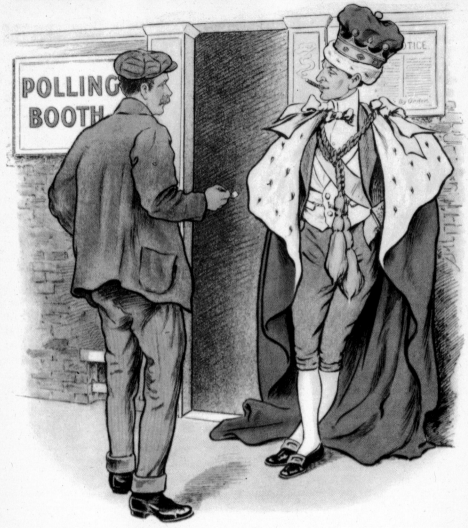

Tory Peer (to Voter): It's all right, my man, you may go and vote if you like, but however you vote, **I** always have the last word.

Why not have the last word yourself?

THE LORDS' VETO QUESTION

Poster published by the Liberal Party, 1910

distinguished Victorian Conservatives like Lecky, failed to take into account. The foggy blurrings of our political landscape assist the repeated transformation scene. Mark how the scene unfolds! First there is a great cheering for the new order—-the tumbrils are trundled out amid a chorus of imprecations on the old order—the band strikes up a chant of the blood-red dawn—the march to the scaffold begins—hurrah! the enemies of the people are about to perish. Then, amid all the confused bustle on this morning of doom, it is suddenly perceived that the gentlemen who were to be driven off in the tumbrils have agilely mounted to the drivers' seats, and are snapping the whip. And, look! as they move forward, the tumbrils themselves seem to be slowly turning into stage-coaches. The revolution has become a Lord Mayor's show. At this, there is renewed cheering from the good-natured populace, who do not seem unduly surprised at the transformation, having seen it all before,.and we bowl along happily to our next revolution. Yet if, in fact, no heads are chopped off, something is usually gained. Some part of the revolution is accepted and tacitly taken over by the other side. Progress can be exasperatingly slow, but consolidation is usually sure.

Grey, the old leader of the Whigs, patient, temperate, unwavering, steered Britain through a revolution, and possibly saved her from a counter-revolution. It certainly wasn't in Grey's mind to attempt to achieve the aims of even the mildest Liberalism at a bound—social reforms, the redress of injustices, the levelling of the grosser inequalities—but he fashioned an instrument of democracy through which in time these ends might be attained. It was upon Grey's last labours that all subsequent achievement was built. The decades after Reform showed a slow but real quickening of humane sensibility in politics. Among good, honest men, there was often to be observed a struggle between fidelity to an infallible theory and the decent inclinations of the heart. Certain well-proved tougheners of the conscience were employed in Parliamentary debate—the arguments that hard cases make bad law, that the destitute are always happier in their condition than they look, and that if good sense once gives way to sentimentality then the skies will come tumbling down. There was another cant phrase much in use—"Men and women cannot be made good by Act of Parliament." Many admirable persons thought this to be a settling answer to the question, "Can't you do more to protect the weak from cruel exploitation?" It was felt that Parliament must not encroach too far into the moral sphere. The Churches, for the most part, warmly agreed. Nor should we forget how strongly held among the respectable was the notion that want, dirt, suffering and the fevers of the slums were spiritual faults. Even Shaftesbury, a saint if ever a man was a saint, obtained little help from organised religion in his early struggles for the child victims of the Industrial Revolution. There was a general feeling, too, that the continuous improvement of the human condition was inevitable under *laissez-faire*, and panegyrists of the age pointed to the rise in living standards and the fall in the death rate that had taken place since the beginning of the century. The truth is that few of the men of that time, even humane men, grasped the size of the Industrial Revolution, or saw that the social problems it brought were too vast in scale to be dealt with by private benevolence. Individual charity could not cope with the mounting evils of the new urban life, of the great submerged masses that had become slaves to the machine. The technology of the age was racing far ahead of its intellectual and moral perceptions. There was also another, and a subtler, change taking place. The illiterate masses in the big centres of population were beginning to look to Government for protection from their masters, and for what nowadays we call economic security. That would have been as incomprehensible an attitude to the eighteenth-century townsman as to the eighteenth-century villager.

A whole complex of religious and moral prejudices had to be broken down before the prosperous middle classes would be willing to contemplate the thought that economic freedoms (as all Parties think of them to-day) were implicit in the idea of Liberty; that industrial democracy was inherent in self-government; and that man's command of his social environment was at least as necessary to his salvation as his command over Nature. Yet at the same time, it was a House of Commons in which Whig aristocrats were in alliance with *laissez-faire* industrialists that passed the first effective Factory Act, the Act which placed a limit upon the hours of work of children under thirteen (1833) and introduced the principle of factory inspection. The Municipal Corporations Act (1835) attacked the rotten boroughs on the civic side. This was the beginning of a genuine local democracy; of town government; and of that devolution of powers which so far has saved Britain from the worst dangers of an over-centralised bureaucracy.

During this phase of its development, however, Liberalism was chiefly conscious of itself as a European force; as the inspiration of constitutional movements abroad; as the destroying angel of autocracy rather than as a dispenser of domestic reform. The average British Liberal of the eighteen-fifties was proud of his country's example in effecting revolutionary changes without shedding blood. In his thoughts, and even more, in his emotions, the triumphs of the Industrial Revolution and the Free Trade age were inseparably linked with his democratic constitution. His was an *outward-looking* Liberalism. Its spirit would, in time, he believed, destroy the old absolutisms in Europe, and replace them by a series of monarchs as constitutional as Queen Victoria, acting solely on the advice of Ministers as sagacious as Peel and Russell, who could be put in, or turned out, at a moment's notice by an ever-vigilant House of Commons, responsible, in turn, only to an omnipotent people. England's word to the world was that there was no more vulgar superstition than that governments derived

LORD PALMERSTON AS PRIME MINISTER ADDRESSING THE HOUSE OF COMMONS
Gladstone, then Chancellor of the Exchequer, is in the foreground:
Disraeli is on the Opposition Front Bench
Engraving after the oil painting by John Phillip, 1860

authority from any supernatural source, or from any sanction except the consent of the governed, though by the governed was usually meant, in those days, "the respectable middle-class interest." The Liberal of this time had a disinterested, romantic interest in nationalism, in self-determination, and in the autonomy of European peoples. His attachment to the liberty of the individual became transferred to the nation in chains, and it was easy for him to behold Italy as a princess of surpassing beauty, languishing in an Austrian dungeon. Her plight was a call to his chivalry. Palmerston, the figure popularly identified with this mood, combined the qualities of Don Quixote and Mr. Podsnap. A survival from the eighteenth century, he had been one of Canning's young men; he had called himself a Liberal-Tory in 1828; he had become Foreign Secretary in Grey's Ministry; and until his death (still Prime Minister) in 1865, whether in jaunty triumph or impenitent disgrace, he represented the outlook of the British middle classes on the world beyond their island. There were two views about Palmerston then, as now; though he has far fewer admirers now than he had then. His prancing diplomacy outraged the Queen;

21

Bright detested and feared his jingoism; but the public at large rejoiced when he snubbed a powerful despot, or broke the rules of the diplomatic game by receiving a deputation of foreign rebels. Throughout the land, inn signs of *The Lord Palmerston* were raised to glorify a sophisticated Saint George with dyed side-whiskers. He could be arrogant, he could be truculent, his conduct on the eve of the Crimean War was unforgivable. But he stood for an England that had grown conscious of her position in the world. She was now so rich and strong she could speak her mind to whom she pleased; and Palmerston knew her mind and spoke it on her behalf. Let the Queen frown, he was Britannia's darling! It proved of enduring value that, despite the bluster and swagger, and the moralisings, this influence was so frequently cast on the side of national freedom against autocracy; that it so often represented an espousal of the weak against the oppressor. So arose the idea of this country as the refuge and hope of free men everywhere in times of persecution. An image of the ideal Britain of the chivalrous heart, sensitive to wrong, sustained the enslaved in the two world wars. A patriot could not wish a happier fate for his country than that she should be identified with the dreams of brave men in other lands; that they should think of her not as their would-be conqueror, but as the guardian of their altars. So long as she stood, their own sacred lamps could not be put out.

There was one further expression of this constitutional Whig-Liberalism. The statesmen of this period laid the base of that commanding structure, the British Commonwealth and Colonial Empire. The Act of 1840 which gave effect to Durham's recommendations of self-government in Canada showed how far ideas on Imperial relationships had advanced since the days of Lord North and the revolt of the American Colonies. The chief credit for this settlement, which showed that the virtues of moderation, tolerance and compromise can sometimes reach heights of prophetic imagination, belonged to the Radical Imperialists of those days. The outstanding figures in this group in the 'thirties and 'forties were Durham ("Radical Jack"), Gibbon Wakefield (whose New Zealand Association made the first settlements in that fertile land, which authority thought unsuited to the white man) and Sir William Molesworth, who had his links with the Chartists. To-day our political parties compete in their professions of attachment to the Commonwealth; and blame one another for past failures to perceive the boundless promise of the relationship. In this day of rediscovery, Durham and Wakefield should not be forgotten. It was at this time, too, that the idea of trusteeship for colonial peoples began to take form. Slavery was abolished throughout the Empire in 1833, but liberal-minded men saw that emancipation must be a continuing process. It was a duty of Government to defend the rights of the natives and, once having freed them from chattel slavery, to spare them from becoming traders' serfs. If a like principle of trusteeship had been laid down on behalf of the children of the cotton towns or the natives of the Potteries how much unhappiness and social strife might Britain have been spared in the nineteenth century.

The India policy that reached its culmination in the transfer of power to the two new Dominions in the summer of 1947 was begun in 1833. The doors were opened to the admission of Indians into responsible positions; Western education was introduced; and the persuasiveness of Macaulay led to the adoption of English as the official tongue. The world now watches the unfolding of Indian destiny to see how closely the reality will compare with Macaulay's dreams of a century and a quarter ago.

GREAT ANTI-SLAVERY MEETING IN EXETER HALL
Water colour by T. H. Shepherd

THE GOLDEN AGE

THE long Whig-Liberal domination was broken by the Conservative Administration of Sir Robert Peel (1841-46). The paradox of Peel is that he was a great Conservative leader who moved steadily from one Liberal position to another, until his followers, all except the most agile of them, lost sight of him. In the end, by his conversion to repeal of the Corn Laws, he ruined the party that his genius had revived. Peel, like Grey, had the art of turning tumbrils into stage-coaches; and the Anti-Corn-Law agitation (1838-46) provided the British people, in a season of distress, with one of their substitutes for barricades and guillotines. Once more, as in the days of Reform, the classes and the masses were brought together, and lifted above themselves, by a cause that promised redemption from more ills than the dear loaf. Cobden and Bright infused the cause with a religious ardour. Chartism weakened as the League strengthened. The old coalition of the 'thirties revived. Town mechanics, farm labourers, manufacturers of the Midlands and the North, and city bankers; Benthamites, and disciples of Adam Smith, Nonconformists, old Whigs, Peelite Tories combined their energies against the landed interest. The country gentlemen in the confusion of their rout found a new champion. By his brilliant rearguard action, Disraeli could not save their cause, but he did avenge them by destroying their lost leader. When Peel fell, Lord John Russell came in—"Finality John," so styled because he was sure that Reform had been settled for good in 1831—Russell, the perfect Whig, outwardly glacial, inwardly suffused by the glow of the "Great and Glorious Revolution" of 1688. It was a wholly different order of revolution which Lord John was invited to lead, a commercial revolution, the inauguration of the era of Free Trade.

In these pinched times, a century later, most of us look back upon the long, golden summer of Free Trade with nostalgia. Britain became the world's forge, workshop, general store and universal provider. Her ships carried her manufactures across all waters. She became the world's banker. She piled up those investments abroad whose loss bears so hardly upon her children to-day. The age was marked by an exhilarating sense of expanding physical energy. Its spirit manifested itself in a hundred daring enterprises and successful hazards—in dazzling strokes of business—in new markets captured—in a thousand mechanical inventions. Population and national wealth multiplied as never before. Is it astonishing that John Bull in 1851, the year of the Great Exhibition, with his pockets full of golden sovereigns, the envy of his neighbours, the despair of his enemies, felt smug, pleased with himself; indeed, the lord of creation? The finest part of the record is that he used his giant's strength on the whole with so much wisdom, generosity and restraint. The Victorians are usually presented as Pecksniffs for sermonising on the moral basis of Free Trade.

It is tempting to make fun of their pretensions. British railway locomotives would open up the jungle; the African savage would cover his nakedness in Lancashire cottons and illuminate his mind with the *Penny Cyclopaedia*; the aborigine of Australia would be blessed by Sheffield steel; and the mysterious Hindu by the Ganges would drink from tin mugs with a Birmingham stamp. Yet we miss the central strength of the Victorian tradition if we dismiss as hypocrisy the idealism that was intertwined with this hearty materialism. Free Trade was seen by our Victorian forefathers as a natural development of Liberalism as a world system. Protective tariffs and monopoly were in their minds bound up with aristocratic privilege and divine right; they were weapons of autocratic governments in the oppression of their peoples. The free exchange of goods would bring prosperity to every land, and, when each nation realised its dependence upon the others, wars would end. Were they, after all, so naïve? Their ghosts might well ask what better world philosophy their children have discovered since.

The real criticism of the politicians of this period is that they failed to come to grips with the domestic problems of individual freedom in an industrial society. The contrast between political vocabulary and social realities gave some of the most illustrious Victorians the appearance of somnambulists muttering incantations as they walk with closed eyes along a cliff edge. Free trade liberated the energies of the middle classes. But in the working classes and the "labouring poor" there resided latent stores of physical and intellectual energy that could not be released for the good of themselves or the whole community through lack of education, lack of health, lack of good drains, and through that squalor of day-to-day existence which drove men and women to the gin palaces. Human labour was regarded as an inexhaustible raw material that could be squandered like coal and iron-ore. It is true that the Governments of this period made some tardy contributions to social reform such as the Public Health Act—Chadwick's reports on sanitation shocked them into action—and they freed the Press from those heavy paper taxes that were commonly known as the taxes on knowledge. It was Disraeli, however, who, in his minority Government in 1867, carried the Second Reform Bill which enfranchised new classes, although it was the sonorous voice of John Bright that had stirred the country. This was the renowned occasion when Disraeli stole the clothes of the Whigs when they had gone bathing.

The future course of Liberalism was to owe far more to the explorations made by the mind of John Stuart Mill (whom Gladstone called "a saint of rationalism") than to all the statesmen of the Victorian age save one, Gladstone himself. Mill lifted the Utilitarian creed to a philosophic height far above Benthamite materialism. He and Gladstone between them transformed Victorian Liberalism from static to dynamic politics. Mill's constant concern was with the nature of Freedom. He saw it as a process of unending revelation. The principles of Liberty were not fixed for ever on the stone tablets of Manchester; they must constantly change with the growth of human society; the eternal spirit ever assuming new shapes, richer, more various and more comprehensive. The evolution of Freedom was the great adventure of man's spirit. Mill taught that the living body of society is deeply hurt by the suffering of its least regarded members. My freedom, and your freedom, said he, is abridged when wrong is done to our fellows. Mill grew ever more disturbed at the prodigious waste of human faculty in an industrial civilisation. The good society could never be built upon a submerged class. Man existed by, and through, his relations with *all* his fellows. Freedom enjoyed by some groups and denied to others was inconsistent with a Liberal State, for it meant that the State itself was in shackles. "No society," he wrote, "in which these liberties are not, on the whole, respected, is free, whatever may be its form of government; and never is completely free in which they do not exist absolute and unqualified." The older Liberals had believed that the function of the State was to hold the ring for the resourceful heroes of Adam Smith, to see fair play between them, but that any restraints beyond this would violate the principles of free enterprise. Mill, however, provided a classic defence for Trade Unionism. He concluded that from the liberty of each individual "follows the liberty, within the same limits, of combination among individuals; freedom to unite, for any purpose not involving harm to others." And he insisted on the State's right to regulate commerce and industry in the interests of individual freedom.

Gladstone was the first nineteenth-century Prime Minister to be born in that century, and when he formed his Government in 1868, it was felt that at last—long past meridian—the new age of nineteenth-century politics had opened. It is customary to describe this Administration as the first purely Liberal government. The Whigs and the Peelites had been absorbed, and Gladstone's alliance with Bright, "the Tribune of the People," was taken as the symbol of the wider alliance between the middle classes and the artisans enfranchised by Disraeli's Act. From 1868 until he laid down the Prime Ministership in 1894, Gladstone held the Liberal Party in his masterful hands. No other man has so dominated a great British party for so long. Longevity was an admired accomplishment of Victorian statesmen. But Gladstone was a contradiction of the almost universal rule that men become more conservative as they grow older. In his youth—the quotation from Macaulay is hackneyed but irresistible—Gladstone was "the rising hope of those stern and unbending Tories." He was an ornament of Peel's great Ministry; he went out of office with his master; advanced from Peelite Conservatism to conservative Liberalism; then, in a majestic pilgrimage through the decades, moved across the variegated terrain of the Liberal Party, leftwards, ever leftwards, until, in his extreme old age, he

A GLADSTONE PAGE.

Drawings by F. C. Gould from *Westminster Populars*, May, 1893

was alarming the young men of his party by his radicalism. There is a story of an old lady, attending a funeral, who heard that Gladstone, then a venerable man, was present. "Oh dear," she sighed, "I do hope he won't create a disturbance *here*." That old lady might represent the Victorian age in its relationship to Gladstone during the latter phases of his career. The older he grew, the greater were the disturbances he created. The Queen was aghast at this violent old man; Disraeli thought him a lunatic. But his portraits, torn out of newspapers, were stuck on their walls by British villagers and Bulgarian peasants, and many of his countrymen, falling under his spell, found their lives changed for ever, as though they had experienced a religious conversion.

Since his death, Gladstone's impetuous spirit has been buried under blocks of memorial masonry. His rival Disraeli, with his imagination, his dazzling wit, his magic of phrase-making, his insight, and his beautifully-contrived theatrical effects, has captured the interest of posterity only too successfully, for he is now regarded almost as some great character in British literature, a glorious figure of fantasy on the scale of Pickwick, Sir Willoughby Patterne, or Mr. Polly, rather than as a great British Prime Minister. Disraeli's "Asian mystery" is like an amusing stage illusion compared with the psychological complexity of Gladstone. Of all the figures of his time Gladstone is the most fascinating, mysterious and original, but he is the one we now see most dimly. Calumny presents him as the prosy embodiment of Victorian hypocrisy; admiration too often produces a marble statue in words, instead of evoking the impassioned, prophetic spirit of a singular genius wrestling with the problems of good and evil on that most treacherous of all battlegrounds, politics.

In politics, the man of imagination and emotional power nearly always cuts a poor figure at the desk, faced by a mound of papers and by the call for continuous decisions, while the good administrator often lacks the vision to see beyond the end of his desk. Gladstone combined in singular degree administrative talents and stormy Old Testament ardours. He had a look of coming down from Sinai and bringing its lightnings and thunders in his hands, and yet, by the old canons, the country never had a more thrifty housekeeper. He is best remembered for his dæmonic indignations—for that "pilgrimage of passion," the Midlothian campaign, whose "drenching rhetoric" so distressed Disraeli—for his crying out against the Bulgarian and Armenian atrocities. Yet how solid and various was his record of legislative achievements. He was four times Prime Minister. In his longer terms of office, particularly in his first Administration, he carried out a number of overdue reforms at a pace till then unknown. Disraeli thought Gladstone an auto-intoxicated hypocrite, while Gladstone regarded Disraeli as an unprincipled adventurer, but Britain profited from their rivalry as from their genius. Gladstone's first Government and Disraeli's six-year Administration, which followed it, were complementary; between them they carried Britain far beyond *laissez-faire*. After they had done their work, there would no longer be any dispute over the principle of using the powers of the State to better the condition of the people. The dispute from now on would be over the *extent* of social organisation that was conceivable in a democracy. Of all that was done by the Gladstone Governments, nothing left so strong a mark as Forster's Education Act of 1870. The provision of a system of compulsory elementary education appeared to the Liberals of that year not only as a setting free of long-buried human talents, but as an assurance of the future well-being of the community. It was only through education and self-discipline — they thought — that democracy could save itself from those elements within it, greed, injustice, and intemperate mob passions, which made for destruction. Sceptical and pessimistic minds likened the Education Act to Prospero teaching Caliban to speak: he would end by cursing his master. The Gladstonian Liberals were, however, optimists about human nature. They believed that Government should be based on a trust of the people, on a faith in the fundamental rightness of their instincts. The Secret Ballot was introduced in 1872, and the agricultural labourer was enfranchised by the Reform Act of 1884.

W. E. FORSTER, 1818-1886
Cartoon by 'Ape' from *Vanity Fair*, 1869

The activities of the Trade Unions were made legal in 1871. But here the reader should be warned that there is an unresolved dispute between Liberals and Conservatives as to whether the subsequent Act of Disraeli's Government was not a more effective piece of law-making than Gladstone's. There is no controversy now, however, on the virtues of Cardwell's army reforms, including the abolition of the purchase of commissions, which met with so fierce a resistance from the military caste that in the end the Royal prerogative had to be invoked; nor over Gladstone's reform of the

29

Civil Service which opened the traditional close preserve of the Tite Barnacles to competitive examination. Much more, indeed, might have been accomplished in the domestic field if it had not been for the vast frustrations of the Irish question which coiled itself around Gladstone like the serpent around the priest in the Laocoon statue. "Romantic Ireland's dead and gone"; the grass has grown over the bloody acres; and the old man's heroic last crusade for Home Rule is forgotten. But, looking back over that waste of blood squandered, and hatreds generated, who now questions if Gladstone was right?

Gladstone's foreign policy was not all of a piece. He usually liked to think of himself as an isolationist, but it was his magnificent interventions that electrified his fellow countrymen from the day when he blazed out against the cruelties of King Bomba of Naples ("the negation of God erected into a system of Government") to his last vehement condemnation of the Turkish massacres. In some of his speeches of the 'seventies one catches a prophetic gleam of the modern ideal of the world society. He was opposed, in turn, to the devil-may-care imperialism of Palmerston, to the Arabian Nights kind of imperialism of Disraeli, and to the smart business man's imperialism of Joseph Chamberlain. The crowds that ran through the London streets chanting, "We don't want to fight, but by Jingo if we do!" paid him the compliment of smashing his windows. He was immoderately abused over Majuba, and over the melancholy fate of Gordon, but what was then considered weakness and vacillation in him derived from an anti-imperialist, conciliatory spirit more in tune with this age than with the 'eighties.

If the test of greatness of a leader is in his power to influence his countrymen to follow the ways of justice and tolerance, to abominate cruelty and to be filled with a generous compassion for its victims, then Gladstone was a very great man. His supreme power resided in his appeal to the individual conscience, in persuading men in the still places of their own hearts to relate temporal things and all "the plausibilities of life" to the eternal. He was a rhetorician, it is true, but, unlike most rhetoricians, he implied more than he said. Not through any system of thought but by his example, by his being what he was in his place and his time, he persuaded men and women to break down inside themselves the old division between politics and their private ethic, between the standards of Government and the standards of personal morality. Because he had lived, men and women found it harder to ask, as they used to ask, when injustice was done, either at home or abroad, "Am I my brother's keeper?" Mill extended the intellectual frontiers of Liberalism, Gladstone its spiritual frontiers; and he gave its chilly logic the warmth and colour of his emotions. The way was prepared for the next advance, even though, immediately after Gladstone's death, the outlook for Liberalism was unpromising, and in his own Party clever and ingenious men, wearied of greatness, appeared to have turned against him.

MODERN LIBERALISM

THE last Liberal Prime Minister of Victoria's reign was "the fascinating failure," Lord Rosebery (1894-95). His brief, unhappy Premiership seemed to mark the exhaustion of Victorian Liberalism. The Party dwindled into opposition and disunity. During the Boer War it was torn by quarrels between its Imperialists and its anti-Imperialists. The Party Leader, Campbell-Bannerman, elated one section of his followers and outraged the other by his Gladstonian denunciation of "methods of barbarism" in the conduct of the war—the concentration camps, the farm burnings. Meanwhile, it seemed to some acute observers that the reaction from Conservative imperialism must inevitably be a militant Socialism. Towards the end of the century, the "Condition of the People" question began to take a foremost place again in men's minds. The idealism of youth was attracted by the poetic Socialism of Ruskin and William Morris. The intelligentsia became fascinated by the social engineering schemes of the Webbs and the Fabians. The Trade Unions awakened to a consciousness of their immense latent political power. The election of Keir Hardie in 1892 as the first Socialist M.P. was a portent, a fiery portent. Change was in the air. How hard-worked was the word New in those days! There was the New Woman, drawn by the comic artists as a strident figure in bloomers, on a bicycle. There was the New Journalism which captured the generation that had been taught to read by the Forster Act. There was the New Drama of Ibsen and Shaw, and there was the Music of the Future of Richard Wagner. There was the New Age of Transport— there were the first high-pooped motor-cars —and, before long, there would be the aeroplane. The lively, original mind of the young H. G. Wells was uniting the most astonishing scientific prophecies with visions of a New Utopia, radiant, hygienic, unparliamentary, which would succeed the hopeless squalor of a competitive and acquisitive society. Wells with his fresh passion, and Shaw with his wit, might between them have seemed sufficient to disrupt a greedy and ugly capitalist order.

LORD ROSEBERY
AS FOREIGN SECRETARY
Drawing by F. C. Gould, 1893

31

'Bradford Declares for Liberalism and Labour'
Drawing of an election procession from the *Illustrated London News*, 1906

The year 1906 was not unlike the year 1830. Once again, out of a great ferment of ideas, with mechanical progress interacting on systems of thought there came a rout of Conservatism and a Liberal triumph. Men who took part in that election have told me that the Liberals were doleful over their chances on the very eve of the polling, but they returned an overwhelming force of 387 Members of Parliament, their majority being the greatest since the Reform Act. Again, as in 1830, Liberalism drew many votes that in times past had been cast regularly for the Tories, and of the men they captured from the other side the most gifted, the most incalculable was the young Conservative M.P. for Oldham, Mr. Winston Churchill. Old sentiments and traditions, as well as the pressure of new forces, were responsible for the Liberal success of 1906. Joseph Chamberlain had split the Conservative Party by his "raging tearing propaganda" for a protection-ist tariff and for the overthrow of the historic Free Trade system. The ghosts of the hungry 'forties were still abroad; and the posters showing the contrast between the big loaf of Free Trade and the little loaf of Protection called up memories of the Anti-Corn-Law League. John Bright had long been dead, but Chamberlain was largely beaten by the influence of his old colleague in the representation of the City of Birmingham. Then again, the conscience of the powerful Nonconformist community had been out-raged by the Conservative Education Act. A number of the most respected members of that very law-abiding community turned up year after year in the Police Courts as "passive resisters" to the payment of the Education Rate, taking their place among the drunks, the petty thieves, the wife-beaters. It may be hard for a young man to-day to comprehend why his father, his intensely respectable father, could be so moved to illegality. To these Nonconformists, the doctrines and rites of the Church of England were abhorrent. That they should pay taxes to support Church schools in which children would be taught a false version of the Christian faith (as their eyes saw it) outraged their deepest feelings. The bright young Tories and the bright young curates, Tory or Christian Socialist, then and later, found the Nonconformist conscience an amusing aberration, but it was unwise to underrate the force of a movement counting among its inspiring geniuses Milton, Bunyan and Wesley. Finally, to complete the tally of causes for the overturn of 1906, the forces of Labour were aroused by the Taff Vale decision of the judges. This decision made a Trade Union collectively responsible for wrongful acts done by any one of its agents. The election brought into the House a group of members who had been put forward by the Labour Representation Committee. They were for the most part working-men Radicals who had the support of the Liberal Party in their constituencies. The Labour Party, as at present constituted, came into being in 1918. It is odd to reflect, looking back across the tides of history, that Labour's Robespierre and Saint-Just forty years ago were thought to be Ramsay MacDonald and Philip Snowden. What ironies the years reveal! These were the very leaders who joined forces with the Tories a quarter of a century later. The new Parliament passed the Trades Disputes Act which annulled Taff Vale. To the bulk of the Liberal Party, exhilarated by its victory, it seemed that Labour would always be a small advance guard, comparable to the Radical M.P.s in the 'thirties and 'forties. It should be

FREE TRADE CARTOON
Drawn for a Liberal election leaflet by F. C. Gould, 1905

said, too, that the left wing of the Liberal Party in this Parliament was adventurously Fabian; went to dinner with the Webbs; and, in after years, some of its members found the transition to Socialism easy.

In our history, that period, from 1906 to 1914, represents the fullest expression or—if that is not too excessive a word—the flowering, of the Liberal tradition. It seemed then—most of all, to the young and hopeful—that the dream of the Liberal State was within reach of fulfilment. It would be a tolerant, free and humane society, its strength perpetually renewed by successive liberations of the energies of the people. Privilege and monopoly would be ended. It would be a peace-loving community. The spread of knowledge would destroy the spell of evil old superstitions and the atavistic passions of the herd. Society would move naturally towards equality, though not towards uniformity. What was the hope? Wherein lay the inspiration of these years? It was that men would in increasing measure behave reasonably towards one another. That their innate sense of injustice would compel them to redress the accumulated social wrongs of the past, the black legacy of the Industrial Revolution. The Liberals of that period were Liberals and could not be Conservatives because they believed Conservatism to be concerned chiefly with the conserving of wealth and privilege—the divine right of the few to govern the many. The bulwark of this privilege was the hereditary principle, a survival of absolutism, and all that was rational in the Liberal mind revolted against the notion that there was a mysterious sanctity and wisdom inherent in the "tenth transmitter of a foolish face."

The Liberals of that period were Liberals and *not* Socialists, because they believed that human progress must be an organic growth ; while Socialism implied a mechanical and regimented society which could have but one end, the Servile State. To the Liberals of that time what mattered most was that Freedom should be put first. They sought to use the social controls, the power of the State, to protect the weak from exploitation, but to release energy, not to fetter it. The Liberal ideal of those years was engulfed by the passions of the first world war, but its inspiration has proved remarkably enduring. In thinking of those times we are not simply indulging in the pleasures of nostalgia. We are not trying to catch the glimmer of ghosts among the ruins. You have only to listen to the debates in the present House of Commons to realise that this period is a living past, not a dead past. The voices of forty years ago are clearly audible in the politics of to-day. Mr. Churchill, as leader of the Conservative Party, is constantly quoting with affectionate approval the flashing rhetoric of the young Mr. Churchill who spoke for Liberalism then, who pleaded for social betterment, defied the Lords, and mocked the gods of Toryism. On the other side, such Labour Front Benchers as Mr. Morrison and Mr. Chuter Ede are steeped in the lore of 1910, and plainly regard themselves as natural inheritors of the Liberal Ministers of that time. The Liberal of

34

DAVID LLOYD GEORGE, 1863–1945

Oil painting by Sir William Orpen, 1927

1948 is, of course, gratified by these manifestations though you must forgive him if sometimes he feels that his own traditions are safest in his own hands. To the young men and women of to-day who are alert and curious about politics, these living echoes of a past beyond the range of their experience must be a little puzzling. It is not putting it too high to say that the foundations of modern Britain were laid in the years before the first world war, but such are the oddities of the teaching of history that many a youth or girl, fresh from the Universities, often knows rather less of this period than of the Wars of the Roses, or of the Chartist times, or the French Revolution.

Leadership is a prime condition for the success of any political movement. The Liberal resurgence of 1906 was fortunate in the notable character of its leaders. Campbell-Bannerman was Prime Minister from the winter of 1905 until 1908; Herbert Henry Asquith succeeded him. Of their Administrations it is common form among modern politicians to say, "How brilliant! What a combination of talents!" How enviable was the Prime Minister who could include in his Cabinet Lloyd George, Winston Churchill, Bryce, Edward Grey as Foreign Secretary, R. B. Haldane at the War Office, John Morley at the India Office, Reginald McKenna, Augustine Birrell, John Burns and Herbert Samuel. It is happily still possible to savour the quality of the Asquith Ministry by listening to two of its distinguished survivors who are active in our political life, Mr. Churchill in the Commons, and Lord Samuel in the House of Lords.

Asquith was a complete embodiment of the Liberalism of that age. He possessed an intellect of massive power and trenchancy. "Send for the sledge-hammer," Campbell-Bannerman used to say when Asquith was needed in hard debate. No man could more effectively demolish sophistry or expose bad logic. Asquith had the breadth of reading and the classical culture of the statesman of the old school. He had the grand manner, he was immensely magnanimous, but he also had a Yorkshire directness. His platform and Parliamentary style was terse, Roman and downright. No man in his Cabinet was a stronger Radical than the Prime Minister, but he had a scorn for demagogic arts. He mistrusted appeals to emotion. He paid an audience the tribute of assuming that it was composed of reasonable, humane and intelligent beings anxious to return a just verdict on the facts of any case. He invested the dusty pursuit of politics with a rare intellectual distinction, and by his example inspired many young men—many of them of parties other than his own—with a high sense of public service. No finer intelligence was ever dedicated to the State in modern times.

The 1906-14 period was one of rapid and far-reaching change. The granting of self-government to the Boers was Campbell-Bannerman's crowning achievement, and it is to him that we owe, more than to any other man, the conception of the British Commonwealth, that most fruitful of developments in world relationships. The Morley-Minto reforms carried

35

RICHARD BURDON HALDANE, SECRETARY OF STATE FOR WAR, 1905-1912
Cartoon by F. C. Gould

India a stage further on the road to home rule. But it was, of course, in the field of domestic reforms that the Campbell-Bannerman and Asquith Governments made their memorable records, and remain of direct interest to us to-day. They faced great issues, and they faced them courageously. This was the time of Britain's New Deal. It provided President Roosevelt, a quarter of a century later, with a pattern and inspiration for his own reforms. The measures carried into law during this term of intense activity included Old Age Pensions, the Miners' Eight Hours Act, Workmen's Compensation, the Children Act, Trade Boards to regulate the sweat shops,

Health Insurance, and the Small Holdings Act. Social security is a commonplace to-day. By comparison with the Beveridge Report, and its effect on modern legislation, these measures may appear mild, cautious first steps, almost non-controversial. We can only appreciate how revolutionary they appeared then by a study of Hansard and the contemporary Press. Henry Chaplin, for example, who had run through two large fortunes, and had been drawing a State pension for years, was shocked at the profligacy of a Government which granted five shillings a week to old men and women to save them from ending their days in the workhouse, and was distressed by the thought that this would discourage the national habit of thrift. The National Health Insurance Bill was denounced as a piece of tyranny, and its opponents grew genuinely moved as they described the humiliations of duch-

SIR HENRY CAMPBELL-BANNERMAN
PRIME MINISTER, 1905-1908
Detail from a cartoon by F. C. Gould

esses forced to lick stamps for their cooks and scullery-maids.

A figure who was at the centre of all these storms was Asquith's Chancellor of the Exchequer, David Lloyd George. He was a son of the people, possessing the imagination and poetry of his race; wonderfully quick-witted, energetic, full of impish humour; irreverent, resilient, and with an enchanter's tongue in conversation and on the platform. In his young manhood he had pitted himself against Welsh squire and parson with Cobbett-like courage, and, like Cobbett, he was a most unphilosophical Radical. Nor since Bright had political Nonconformity produced such a spokesman. The Chancellor of the Exchequer who from the Treasury

37

Bench described the august Cecils as coming down to the House of Commons with "hands dripping with the fat of sacrilege," and poked outrageous fun at dukes, enjoyed making enemies, and did not at all mind being called a cad by the nobility and gentry. Some of those who admired his qualities felt that his hold on principles was light; that he was moved less by ideas than by instincts; but he knew in his bones what it was like to be poor.

Although, as we have seen, the Liberal Party was returned by an unprecedented majority at the 1906 elections, the House of Lords declined to accept the popular verdict. Very early in the life of that Parliament, the Peers began to reject or to amend Government measures. Augustine Birrell's Education Bill, which sought to redress the grievances of the Nonconformists, was mauled out of all recognition and had to be abandoned. A Bill to curtail Plural Voting—in those days a man of property might have votes in a dozen or more constituencies—was summarily flung out by the Lords. They rejected, too, a Licensing Bill which sought to reduce the number of public houses. The Miners' Eight Hours Bill was subjected to amendments, and other Government legislation was mutilated by the busy Peers. This constant butchery created a mounting resentment. What was insufferable to the Liberals was the sublime assumption of the Tory Lords that their prerogatives should override the popular will.

The climax came when the Second Chamber took the great decision to throw out the Budget of 1909. The Government had been forced to cast around for fresh sources of revenue. Social reforms had to be paid for, as increased armaments had to be paid for. It must be remembered that during these years the German threat was steadily darkening over Europe. Large sums were needed for the Army and the Fleet. When the fatal day did come in 1914, the country might thank its stars for the preparations that had been made by Haldane, that model of efficiency as War Minister, and for Mr. Churchill's vigilant direction at the Admiralty. The "People's Budget" of 1909 imposed heavier taxes on the rich, and, in particular, on the landlords. The Chancellor (Lloyd George) proposed a duty on undeveloped land, a tax on coal royalties, increased liquor duties, a rise in death duties, and super-tax on incomes beyond £5,000 a year. Measured by present-day standards of taxation, these proposals were gentle indeed, but they aroused a storm of wrath. This was "pillage," "brigandage," "confiscatory Socialism." The land tax shocked and alarmed the aristocratic houses. It seemed to strike at the very roots of their powers and privileges. The House of Lords, the stronghold of the great landlords, rejected the Budget, an action that violated all constitutional practice. Asquith had no choice but to go to the country on the issue of Peers versus People. In the elections of January 1910 the Liberal strength was considerably reduced, but the support of the Irish Party and the Labour members gave the Government a majority of 124 in the new Parliament. In the spring of that year, the Budget was accepted in sullen silence by the Upper House and Asquith

THE NATIONAL HEALTH INSURANCE BILL
Lloyd George as Chancellor of the Exchequer receives a deputation at the Treasury
Drawing by Frédéric de Haenen from the *Illustrated London News*, December 2nd, 1911

introduced the Parliament Bill to curb the powers of their Lordships. Then, in May, King Edward VII died. An effort to reach a truce in the struggle between the parties failed, and a second election on the issue of the Lords' veto became inevitable. In this contest, which took place in December 1910, the balance of parties remained almost unchanged, and the conflict between the two Houses was resumed with increased sharpness. The Parliament Bill sought to abolish the Lords' veto on Money Bills and to ordain that any other legislation passed by the Commons in three successive sessions—meaning a period of two years—should automatically become law over their Lordships' heads. This measure was severely amended by the Upper House. Asquith served brusque notice that unless the Parliament Bill was accepted in its unamended form, the Government would advise the King to create a sufficient number of Peers to carry it. The King, he added, had signified his readiness to act on that advice. The threat to swamp their Lordships' House with four hundred new creations brought about a cleavage among the Tory peers—between those who were prepared to "die in the last ditch," under the leadership of the venerable former Lord Chancellor, Halsbury, and the moderates, led by Lansdowne and Curzon, who were in favour of making a solemn remonstrance—and then abstaining from voting. There had been no such issue as the Parliament Act to convulse our politics since the Reform Bill. Tempers were high, the atmosphere feverish. In the decisive division—on whether the Peers would insist on their Amendments—the Government majority was narrow: seventeen. It was the votes of the Bishops that saved their Lordships from dying in the last ditch. This struggle was in essence a renewal of the old fight for power between the landed interest and the middle classes and working classes which had been waged over Reform in 1830-31 and over the Corn Laws in 1846. It was a significant part of this historical development that Lloyd George turned his energies to agrarian reform, to a Land Campaign that was a frontal attack on the evils of landlordism. In the cities and rural areas alike he set great audiences singing, "God gave the land to the people!"

After the passing of the Parliament Act in 1911, the powers of the Lords remained a sleeping issue until the autumn of 1947 when the Labour Government chose to awaken it. But the Parliament Act did not allay the violence of party spirit. Far from it. The years just before the first world war were marked by exasperated nerves, by explosions of irrational fury and a hankering after direct action. The violence which attended some of the labour disputes of the period was a manifestation of the spirit of the age. The Conservatives led the revolt from reason and adopted what Asquith called "the grammar of anarchy." The supple and graceful dialectician, Mr. Arthur Balfour, was replaced as their leader by the angular Mr. Bonar Law. The great storm centre was the Irish Home Rule Bill. This Bill, like the Welsh Disestablishment measure, became law in 1914 under the Parliament Act, having been passed in three successive sessions, but, owing to the war, its operation was suspended. The "Ulster Rebellion" led by Sir Edward Carson, and supported with enthusiasm by the Tory Party, represented a challenge to ordered Government quite without parallel in our modern history. Nowadays, when one reads the fantastic accounts of those days in the yellowing newspaper files—the lawless behaviour of eminent lawyers, the incitements to sedition by elder statesmen, the gun-running, the solemn covenant taken to resist the Government, the "mutiny at the Curragh," the fierce speeches, the mad actions—one has to stop and say, "Oh, really, now, this can't be the England we were brought up in. These queer irrational characters can have no conceivable connection with the England we live in to-day." One of Mr. Bonar Law's messages

HERBERT HENRY ASQUITH, PRIME MINISTER 1908-1916
Detail from an oil painting by Sir William Orpen, 1910

to Sir Edward Carson read, "Whatever steps you may feel compelled to take, whether they are constitutional, or whether in the long run they are unconstitutional, you have the whole Unionist Party, under my leadership, behind you." If the first world war had not broken out in August 1914, it is hard to see how civil war could have been averted. The Ulstermen were arming on one side of the border, the Irish Nationalists on the other. In Britain, the bitterness between the Parties was more ominous than it had been since the Reform Bill.

THE PARTY AND THE PRESENT

THE passions of war are destructive of the values of Liberalism. The 1914-18 conflict represented a total overthrow of the old Liberal hopes of a world in which swords would be beaten into plough-shares, and the free exchange of goods and ideas lead to a co-operative commonwealth of the nations. In addition, the Party was badly split over personalities. The circumstances under which Mr. Lloyd George replaced Mr. Asquith as the War Prime Minister in 1916 created a long-enduring schism. Nothing is more distasteful than to revive the memory of bygone feuds, and to a generation that had no part in them they must appear extremely uninteresting. Suffice it to say, that the divisions in the Party led to a disastrous result at the General Election of 1918, the "Khaki Election," at the end of the war. The coalition of Mr. Lloyd George's Liberal and Conservative supporters swept the country, and the Asquith Liberals were reduced to 34 members, their leader, together with many former Ministers, being defeated.

Looking back now on the two decades of decay between the wars, he would be a tough and indurated partisan indeed who still rejoiced at that shattering of the Liberal Party. In 1922 the Coalition collapsed, and in the ensuing elections 64 Independent Liberals and 53 National (Lloyd Georgian) Liberals were returned. A year later Mr. Baldwin, who had succeeded Mr. Bonar Law as Prime Minister, sought a mandate for Protection as his way out of the nation's mounting economic troubles. That challenge to Free Trade sentiment united the followers of Mr. Asquith and Mr. Lloyd George, and in the 1923 elections 158 Liberals were returned, the Party polling 4,300,000 votes to Labour's 4,500,000 and Conservatism's 5,500,000. Labour had 192 members and the Conservatives 258. On the country's verdict, the Liberals had no choice but to declare against Mr. Baldwin's Government on the motion of "no confidence," and this inevitably meant that Mr. Ramsay MacDonald, as leader of the Labour Party, was called upon to form a Government. In that brief Parliament, the Liberals were treated by Mr. MacDonald, sometimes with contempt, often with irritation, as "patient oxen," and, within eleven months, a muddled and obscure incident over the prosecution of a Communist newspaper led to another dissolution. In the ensuing election, the voters were stampeded by the melodramatic "Red Letter" scare, a supposed intervention by Mr. Zinoviev of the Comintern in British politics. The Liberals were the chief casualties in this confused struggle, losing 116 seats.

During the General Strike of 1926, the breach between Mr. Asquith and Mr. Lloyd George was unhappily opened again. In 1928, Asquith, who had become Lord Oxford, died. With him there passed the distinction and amplitude of the Victorian tradition in politics. During the General Election of 1929, Mr. Lloyd George conducted a vigorous campaign on a

LORD BEVERIDGE
Oil painting by Sir William Nicholson, 1926

policy of conquering unemployment. The Party very substantially increased its vote, but "it was tripped on the triangle" of our unrepresentative electoral system. Once again, a minority Labour Government came into office under Mr. MacDonald. In all these contests the Party's strength in the constituencies was most inadequately reflected in its representation in the House of Commons. In this 1929 election, for example, the Conservatives with 8,600,000 votes secured 260 seats, Labour with 8,300,000 votes 288 seats, and the Liberals with 5,300,000 votes only 59 seats. But one thing, at least, was impossible. A Liberal Party with so large a following in the country could not be ignored. The other parties, in office or in opposition, showed themselves very conscious of its existence.

The influence of the Party was greatly enhanced by the fact that a number of men of high ability, excluded by the caprices of the electoral system from the House of Commons, found an alternative means of serving the State by engaging upon group studies of the nation's chief problems. One of the most striking and fruitful of these was *Britain's Industrial Future*, the Yellow Book of 1928, which has not only had a marked influence on the evolution of Liberal ideas on the economic structure, but has been drawn upon by the other Parties. It is one of the services of Liberalism that it provided a national "Brains Trust" in the fallow years between the wars. What modern politician has not quarried in the Yellow Book, or in *We Can Conquer Unemployment*, or does not owe a great deal to the creative ideas of Lord Beveridge?

When the acute economic crisis of 1931 brought about the downfall of the second Labour Government, the Liberals joined Mr. MacDonald's Coalition, Mr. Lloyd George, then in ill health, remaining aloof. They returned 72 members in that landslide election in which Labour's seats were reduced to 52. Those Liberals who followed Sir Herbert Samuel (now Lord Samuel) ultimately resigned from the Coalition over the Ottawa agreements, which ran counter to their Free Trade principles. Those who adhered to the leadership of Sir John Simon (now Lord Simon) stayed in the Government. In the election of 1935, won by Mr. Baldwin on the pledge to support the League of Nations and the system of collective security, the Liberals returned 21 members and the Liberal Nationals (Simonites) 33. During the years of deepening shadow before the war, Liberal opinion exerted an influence far greater than its shrunken strength in the House of Commons might imply. The Party had always put the League in the forefront of its foreign policy. In these anxious years it spent a great deal of its energies in advocating the creation of a collective system that would check aggressors. The explosion of anger which destroyed the Hoare-Laval Pact (the recognition of Mussolini's conquest of Abyssinia) showed the strength of Liberal sentiment in the country. Like Mr. Churchill, the Liberals were unswervingly opposed to the policy of appeasement, and they did not share the illusions of Munich.

When war came in 1939, the Liberal Party declined to join Mr. Neville Chamberlain's Government from lack of confidence in his leadership. They voted against him in the crucial debate on the conduct of the Norway campaign, and when Mr. Churchill formed his Coalition in May 1940, Sir Archibald Sinclair, their Parliamentary leader, and other members of the Party took office. The Liberals, together with the Socialists, withdrew their support of the Coalition after the surrender of Germany, as they were opposed to carrying into peace a union of parties designed solely to achieve the winning of the war. The post-war troubles of the nation would be many; the cures offered by the parties widely differed; the Liberals believed the people should make their choice between them. Mr. Churchill formed his Caretaker Government, and appealed to the country. In his election speeches, the Prime Minister showed some indignation at the Liberal attitude, reproaching them for deserting the old cause of freedom now imperilled by Socialism. The elections astonished most people by the extent of the Conservative losses, and Mr. Attlee was able to form the first Labour Government based on a clear, indeed a very large, majority in the House, though Labour was in a minority of the total votes polled. The Liberals were placed at a heavy disadvantage in the competition of parties. Running 307 candidates, and polling 2,239,668 votes, they succeeded in returning no more than 12 M.P.s. Sir Archibald Sinclair and a number of members of long service were defeated. The Party set to work with good heart to repair its losses and to reaffirm its independence. Within a week or two of its defeat, it set a goal of 600 candidates at the next election. It gave much time to strengthening its machinery and finances. And at the Assembly of the Party at Bournemouth in 1947 it produced a comprehensive statement of policy. The present (1948-49) President of the Party organisation is Mr. Elliott Dodds. His immediate predecessor was Mr. Isaac Foot, who in turn succeeded Lady Violet Bonham-Carter, daughter of the late Lord Oxford. The Chairman of the Executive is Mr. Philip Fothergill. That the Parliamentary Party, so reduced in numbers, has been able to make a spirited contribution to debate owes much to the leadership of Mr. Clement Davies and to the tireless vigilance of the Chief Whip, Colonel Frank Byers.

The Liberal Party gives every active member a voice in the conduct of his Party's affairs. The Party organisation is composed of the Assembly, the Council, the Area Federations and the Constituency Associations. The constituency associations represent the grass-roots. These local bodies adopt the candidates and each of them is responsible for its own working arrangements, for raising funds, and for maintaining an agent. The Liberals must look to the shillings and pennies of their rank-and-file for financial support. Everyone who pays an annual subscription to the Association in his constituency, or to such branches of it as a Women's Liberal Association, a Young Liberal League or a Ward Association, is a member of the

THE RIGHT HON. CLEMENT DAVIES, K.C., M.P.
Cartoon by J. Ross, 1948

Constituency body and of the Party, and so has a share in its fortunes. Such schemes as the threepence-a-week fund subscribed through the *Liberal News* are examples of adaptation to necessity by a Party which has no vested interests to sustain it. The constituency associations are joined together in Area Federations. One of the major tasks of these Federations in late years has been to revive constituency associations in districts where none has existed for a long time. The policy-making body of the Party is the Assembly—composed of representatives of the constituency associations and of affiliated organisations, Liberal members of both Houses of

Parliament, and candidates. The Assembly must meet at least once a year. The Council of the Party, whose function is to apply a constant stimulus to Liberal effort, consists of a number of members elected by the Assembly and others representing the several branches of the Party. The Council is responsible for raising and administering the funds of the Party, appoints its Chairman and Executive Committee, issues statements giving the Liberal attitude to events of the day, and is in charge of the national publicity of the Party. The National Executive Committee is a compact body which meets at least once a month and is responsible for the everyday working of the Party. The Liberal Party Committee is the "Shadow Cabinet" and consists of the leader of the Liberal M.P.s in the House of Commons, the Chief Whip, the Leader of the Liberal Peers, the President of the Party Organisation, the Chairman of the National Executive, the Chairman (or other representative) of the Liberal Candidates' Association, and twelve additional members appointed by the Leader of the Party in agreement with the President of the Party Organisation from a nominated panel of forty.

What are the aims of Liberalism to-day? The preamble to the Party's constitution defines its goal in these words : "The Liberal Party exists to build a Liberal Commonwealth, in which every citizen shall possess liberty, property and security, and none shall be enslaved by poverty, ignorance or unemployment. Its chief care is for the rights and opportunities of the individual, and in all spheres it sets freedom first." The Statement of Policy which emanated from the Party in the summer of 1947 gives the Liberal point of view on the main topics of foreign, domestic and Imperial concern. There is no space in this brief sketch to touch on all sections of this carefully elaborated programme, ranging from colonial policy to health and housing, from the future of agriculture to House of Lords reform. Within this framework, however, one may draw attention to certain aspects of the Policy Statement which bring the Liberal attitude most sharply into contrast with that of the other two Parties. On foreign affairs, the Statement pledges the Party to work to strengthen the United Nations and proposes modifying or abolishing the veto power. It affirms its enduring belief in Free Trade. Full employment and high wages in Britain—states the Party—depend upon the expansion of world commerce, and so this country should take the lead in breaking down the barriers. It is recognised that as things are, all controls on international trade cannot be lifted at once, but a Liberal Government would aim first at abolishing protective tariffs on food and the raw materials of agriculture and industry, and, afterwards, at repealing all other protective tariffs in five annual instalments. The Party favours the ideal of a United Europe, within the frame of the United Nations, and sees the "functional approach" as the most effective and practical one, that is the creation of a European transport system and other instruments of common economic interest. On National Defence, the Party takes the line

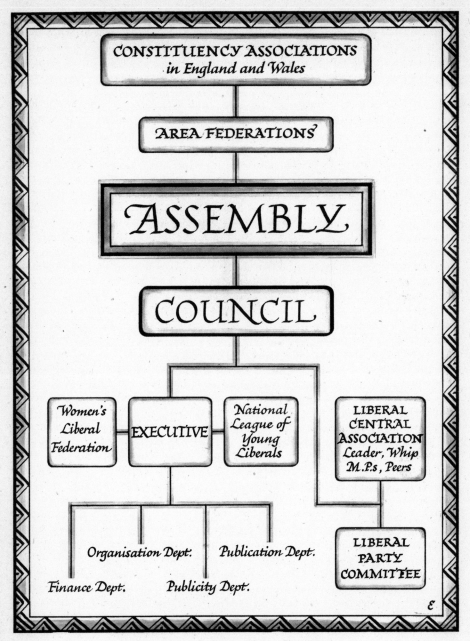

CONSTITUENCY ASSOCIATIONS
in England and Wales

AREA FEDERATIONS

ASSEMBLY

COUNCIL

Women's
Liberal
Federation

EXECUTIVE

National
League of
Young
Liberals

LIBERAL
CENTRAL
ASSOCIATION
Leader, Whip
M.P.s, Peers

Organisation Dept.

Publication Dept.

Finance Dept.

Publicity Dept.

LIBERAL
PARTY
COMMITTEE

CHART OF THE LIBERAL PARTY ORGANISATION

that conscription is not a good thing in itself, nor desirable as a permanent institution in this country. It thinks the time has come for the three services to be fused; and for a fresh thinking-out of all the problems of defence in the light of the new discoveries of science, among which atomic energy stands first.

Those parts of the Policy Statement which deal with labour and industry will obviously take a foremost place on the platforms during the current period of economic crisis. The Liberals fix their hopes on an ever-widening democracy in industry. They take their stand on Full Employment in a Free Society, are opposed to direction of labour, and ask for a national wages policy as "an indispensable requisite for social justice and industrial peace." The general cry to-day is for more production. But how to get it? It is a strong Liberal argument that if the workers are treated merely as hands they cannot be expected to put forth their fullest efforts or to abandon those restrictive practices which hamper output. Statutory Works Councils, they think, should be set up in all concerns employing more than 200 persons; and it should be an obligation upon every employer to lay before the Works Council at regular intervals a statement as to the trading conditions of the firm, and, in the case of public limited-liability companies, to produce and explain the balance-sheet once a year. It has been a long-standing Liberal policy to extend co-partnership and profit-sharing so that the largest possible number of employees may eventually have a very real stake in the enterprise in which they are engaged. "Ownership for All" is the ultimate goal of Liberal social and economic policy. Liberalism does not seek the destruction of private property, but its better diffusion. The spread of individual ownership is "the only alternative to State monopoly or private monopoly." The Party's object is "to abolish the proletariat and make all men owners. . . ." "It is with this belief and this ultimate aim that it advocates the reward of effort, the industrial freedom of the worker, his close integration with the undertaking in which he works, his growing participation in profits and a high standard of wages; the disestablishment of private monopoly and the abolition of the restrictive practices of both capital and labour; a taxation policy which shall be directed towards rewarding effort and encouraging initiative." As for the Trade Unions, the Party believes that every facility should be given them to recruit members by persuasion and attraction, but it condemns completely the exercise of compulsion and pressure to force workers to join a union—or one particular union. Liberals regard "contracting out" of the political levy as a form of social coercion and would restore "contracting in" as essential to political and personal freedom. They call for a Royal Commission to investigate the present position of Trade Unionism in relation to industry, production and politics. A Liberal Government would take strong action against monopolies, trade associations and amalgamations which stifle production and breed restrictive practices.

Liberals are "inexorably opposed to collective ownership of all the means of production, distribution and exchange" for it will, they say, neither increase the flow of goods and services the country so badly needs nor will it maintain the Free Society. No undertaking or industry should be nationalised until it has been sufficiently demonstrated by an impartial scientific inquiry that State control is necessary in the interests of the community as a whole, that control without State ownership is not feasible, and that State ownership can be expected so to increase productive efficiency as to outweigh the disadvantages inherent in it.

One of the most characteristic developments in modern Liberalism is expressed in a section of the Policy Statement which bears the somewhat forbidding title, "Machinery of Government." What Walt Whitman called "the never-ending audacity of elected persons" becomes an increasing threat as Government takes ever-larger authority over the community. There is a top-heavy concentration of power in Whitehall. "Centralisation," to employ an ugly word, has grown, is growing, and should be diminished. This rush of blood to the head is bad for the country; it is not in keeping with the nature of the British people; and with the way in which they like to run their affairs. Among the distinctive attributes of this country are the vigour of its regional life and the tenacity of its local genius. To roll all power up into a ball in Whitehall offends against the national spirit. Liberalism would give to the people of Scotland and Wales greater control of their own affairs by setting up Scottish and Welsh legislative bodies. They would reduce to a minimum the power of Ministers to legislate by regulations and Orders in Council, that dangerous growth which makes a mockery of democratic government. The Liberals, who have suffered more than any other party from our unrepresentative electoral system are in favour of Fair Voting—by the single transferable vote, the simplest form of proportional representation.

What of the future? On the morrow of the Gravesend, Howdenshire and East Edinburgh elections, the *Daily Herald* said that the inescapable conclusion for Liberals was that they must join the Labour Party to achieve the realisation of their ideals. In the same week of November 1947 the Liberal Party issued a strong declaration of independence, signed by its leaders and principal officers. This statement denounced the campaign being pursued by the Conservative Central Office in all parts of the country to undermine Liberal organisations, and create an anti-Socialist front. "The only effect of a fusion between Liberals and Conservatives would be to consolidate the Socialists in power," said the signatories, and they pledged themselves to "fight on—sustained by the conviction that a world in which the voice of independent Liberalism is not heard must inevitably end in disaster." The fortune-tellers of politics gaze into very cloudy crystals these days. There are rumours of strains inside both the Conservative and Labour Parties, of divisions between their left and right wings. In this time of doubt and confusion the continued independent existence of British Liberalism seems more than ever important. There are increasing numbers of people in this country who are unhappy at the drift towards the total State and yet have no faith in Conservatism. It is, says the Liberal, vital that the nation should have an alternative to dogmatic Socialism which is not the old-fashioned Conservatism that brought Britain to so sorry a pass in the years between the wars. He believes that the existence of his Party saved the country from a ruinous class struggle in Victorian times. He is confident that the principles of Liberalism can be applied with equal success to the social problems and the technological problems of the present age.

SHORT BIBLIOGRAPHY

An Inquiry into the Nature and Causes of the Wealth of Nations by Adam Smith. 1776 (1933, Everyman's Library).—*On Liberty* by J. S. Mill. 1859 (1946, Blackwell).—*The Life of William Ewart Gladstone* by Viscount Morley. 3 vols. 1903, Macmillan.—*Liberalism* by L. T. Hobhouse. 1911 (Home University Library).—*Britain's Industrial Future: being the report of the Liberal Industrial Inquiry.* 1928.—*Life of Lord Oxford and Asquith* by J. A. Spender and Cyril Asquith. 2 vols. 1932, Hutchinson.—*War Memoirs* by David Lloyd George. 6 vols. 1933-36, Nicholson & Watson.—*A History of the Liberal Party* by Sir Henry Slesser. 1944, Hutchinson.—*Full Employment in a Free Society* by Lord Beveridge. 1944, Allen & Unwin.—*Memoirs* by Viscount Samuel. 1945, Cresset Press